THE CASE OF WAGNER

and

NIETZSCHE CONTRA WAGNER

By FRIEDRICH NIETZSCHE

Translated by THOMAS COMMON

A Digireads.com Book
Digireads.com Publishing

The Case of Wagner and Nietzsche Contra Wagner
By Friedrich Nietzsche
Translated by Thomas Common
ISBN 10: 1-4209-4880-6
ISBN 13: 978-1-4209-4880-6

Please visit *www.digireads.com*

CONTENTS

THE CASE OF WAGNER:

A MUSICIAN'S PROBLEM: BEING A LETTER FROM TURIN, MAY 1888

ridendo dicere severum . . . .

PREFACE

I relieve myself a little. It is not solely out of sheer wickedness that I praise Bizet at the expense of Wagner in this work. In the midst of much pleasantry, I bring forward a case which is serious enough. It was my fate to turn the back on Wagner; to be fond of aught afterwards was a triumph. No one, perhaps, had been more dangerously entangled in Wagnerism, no one has defended himself harder against it, no one has been more glad to get rid of it. A long history!—Is there a word wanted for it?—If I were a moralist, who knows how I should designate it! Perhaps *self-overcoming.*—But the philosopher never loves moralists . . . neither does he love fancy words . . .

What does a philosopher firstly and lastly require of himself? To overcome his age in himself, to become "timeless." With what, then, has he to wage the hardest strife? With the characteristics in which he is just the child of his age. Well! I am the child of this age, just like Wagner, *i.e.* a *décadent;* I am, however, conscious of it; I defended myself against it. My philosophic spirit defended itself against it.

The problem of *décadence* is, in fact, that which has occupied me most profoundly;—I have had reasons for it. "Good and Evil" is only a variety of that problem. When one has learned to discern the symptoms of decline, one also understands morality,—one understands what conceals itself under its holiest names and valuation-formulae; namely, *impoverished* life, desire for the end, great lassitude. Morality *negatives* life . . . For such a task I required some self-discipline:—I had to engage in combat *against* whatever was morbid in me, including Wagner, including Schopenhauer, including all modern "humanity."—A profound estrangement, coolness, and sobriety with reference to everything temporary or opportune; and as my highest wish, the eye of *Zarathushtra,* an eye, which, exalted to an immense height, surveys the whole phenomenon of man,—looks *down* on it . . . To attain such an object—what sacrifice would not be appropriate? What "self-overcoming!" What "self-denying!"

My most important experience was a *convalescence;* Wagner belongs only to my maladies.

Not that I would wish to be ungrateful to this malady. If in this work I maintain the proposition that Wagner is *hurtful,* I want none the less to maintain *to whom,* in spite of it all, Wagner is indispensable—to the philosopher. In other departments people may perhaps get along without Wagner; the philosopher, however, is not free to dispense with him.

The philosopher has to be the bad conscience of his time; for that purpose he must possess its best knowledge. But where would he find a better initiated guide for the labyrinth of modern soul, a more eloquent psychological expert than Wagner? Modernism speaks its *most familiar* language in Wagner: it conceals neither its good nor its evil, it has lost all its sense of shame. And reversely: when one has formed a clear notion about what is good and evil in Wagner, one has almost determined the *value* of modernism.—I understand perfectly, when a musician says now, "I hate Wagner, but I no longer stand any other music." I should however also understand a philosopher who declared, "Wagner *summarises* modernism. There is no help for it; we must first be Wagnerians"...

1

I heard yesterday—will you believe it?—the masterpiece of *Bizet* for the twentieth time. I again held out with meek devotion, I again succeeded in not running away. This victory over my impatience surprises me. How such a work perfects one! One becomes a "masterpiece" one's self by its influence.—And really, I have appeared to myself, every time I have heard *Carmen,* to be more of a philosopher, a better philosopher than at other times: I have become so patient, so happy, so Indian, so *sedate* . . . Five hours sitting: the first stage of holiness! May I venture to say that Bizet's orchestra music is almost the sole orchestration I yet endure? That *other* orchestra music which is all the rage at present, the Wagnerian orchestration, at once brutal, artificial, and "innocent"—thereby speaking to the three senses of modern soul at the same time,—how detrimental to me is that Wagnerian orchestration! I call it the Sirocco. An unpleasant sweat breaks out on me. My good time is at an end.

This music seems to me to be perfect. It approaches lightly, nimbly, and with courtesy. It is amiable, it does not produce *sweat.* "What is good is easy; everything divine runs with light feet:"—the first proposition of my Æsthetics. This music is wicked, subtle, and fatalistic; it remains popular at the same time,—it has the subtlety of a race, not of an individual. It is rich. It is precise. It builds, it organises, it completes; it is thus the antithesis to the polypus in music, "infinite melody." Have more painful, tragic accents ever been heard on the stage? And how are they obtained? Without grimace! Without counterfeit coinage! Without the *imposture* of the grand style! Finally, this music takes the auditor for an intelligent being, even for a musician; here also Bizet is the contrast to Wagner, who, whatever else he was, was certainly the *most uncourteous* genius in the world. (Wagner takes us just as if ——, he says a thing again and again until one despairs,—until one believes it.)

And once more, I become a better man when this Bizet exhorts me. Also a better musician, a better *auditor.* Is it at all possible to listen better?—I bury my ears *under* this music, I hear the very reason of it. I seem to assist at its production—I tremble before dangers which accompany any hazardous enterprise, I am enraptured by strokes of good fortune of which Bizet is innocent.—And, curiously enough, I don't think of it after all, or I don't *know* how much I think of it. For quite other thoughts run through my mind at the time . . . Has it been noticed that music *makes* the spirit *free?* that it gives wings to thought? that one becomes so much more a philosopher, the more one becomes a musician?—The grey heaven of abstraction thrilled, as it were, by lightnings; the light strong enough for all the filigree of things; the great problems ready to be grasped; the universe surveyed as from a mountain summit.—I have just defined philosophical pathos.—And *answers* fall into my lap unexpectedly; a little hail-shower of ice and wisdom, of *solved* problems . . . Where am I? Bizet makes me productive. All that is good makes me productive. I have no other gratitude, nor have I any other *proof* of what is good.

2

This work saves also; Wagner is not the only "Saviour." With Bizet's work one takes leave of the *humid* north, and all the steam of the Wagnerian ideal. Even the dramatic action saves us therefrom. It has borrowed from Mérimée the logic in passion, the shortest route, *stern* necessity. It possesses, above all, what belongs to the warm climate, the dryness of the air, its *limpidezza*. Here, in all respects, the climate is altered. Here a different sensuality expresses itself, a different sensibility, a different gaiety. This music is gay; but it has not a French or a German gaiety. Its gaiety is African; destiny hangs over it, its happiness is short, sudden, and without forgiveness. I envy Bizet for having had the courage for this sensibility, which did not hitherto find expression in the cultured music of Europe—this more southern, more tawny, more scorched sensibility . . . How the yellow afternoons of its happiness benefit us! We contemplate the outlook: did we ever see the sea *smoother?* And how tranquillisingly the Moorish dance appeals to us! How even our insatiability learns for once to be satiated with its lascivious melancholy! Finally, love,—love retranslated again into *nature! Not* the love of a "cultured maiden!" No Senta-sentimentality![1] But love as fate, as *fatality,* cynical, innocent, cruel,—and thus true to *nature!* Love, which in its expedients is the war of the sexes, and in its basis their *mortal hatred.*—I know of no case where tragic humour, which forms the essence of love, has expressed itself so strenuously, has formulated itself so terribly, as in the last cry of Don Jose, with which the work concludes:

> "Yes! *I myself* have killed her;
> Oh my Carmen! my Carmen adored!"

—Such a conception of love (the only one which is worthy of a philosopher) is rare; it distinguishes a work of art among thousands of others. For, on an average, artists do like all the world, or worse even—they *misunderstand* love. Wagner also has misunderstood it. People imagine they are unselfish in love because they seek the advantage of another being, often in opposition to their own advantage. But for so doing they want to *possess* the other being . . . Even God himself is no exception to this rule. He is far from thinking, "What need you trouble about it, if I love you?"—he becomes a terror, if he is not loved in return. *L'Amour*—with this word one gains one's case with gods and men—*est de tous les sentiments le plus égoïste, et, par conséquent, lorsqu'il est blessé, le moins généreux* (B. Constant).

3

You already see how much this music *improves* me?—*Il faut méditerraniser la musique:* I have reasons for using this formula (*Beyond Good and Evil,* Nr. 255). The return to nature, to health, to gaiety, to youth, and to *virtue!*—And yet I was one of the most corrupt of the Wagnerians . . . I was capable of taking Wagner seriously . . . Ah, this old magician! to what extent has he imposed upon us! The first thing his art furnishes is a magnifying-glass. We look into it, we don't trust our eyes—everything becomes great, *even Wagner becomes great* . . . What a wise rattlesnake! All his life he has rattled before

---

[1] Senta is one of Wagner's female personages.

us about "devotion," about "loyalty," about "purity;" with a panegyric on chastity, he withdrew from the *corrupt* world!—And we have believed him . . .

But you do not listen to me? You prefer even the *problem* of Wagner to that of Bizet? I don't undervalue it myself, it has its charm. The problem of salvation is even a venerable problem. There is nothing which Wagner has meditated on more profoundly than salvation; his opera is the opera of salvation. Someone always wants to be saved in Wagner's works; at one time it is some little man, at another time it is some little woman—that is *his* problem.—And with what opulence he varies his leading motive! What rare, what profound sallies! Who was it but Wagner taught us that innocence has a preference for saving interesting sinners (the case in *Tannhäuser*)? Or that even the Wandering Jew will be saved, will become *settled,* if he marries (the case in the *Flying Dutchman*)? Or that corrupt old women prefer to be saved by chaste youths (the case of *Kundry* in *Parsifal*)? Or that young hysterics like best to be saved by their doctor (the case in *Lohengrin*)? Or that handsome girls like best to be saved by a cavalier who is a Wagnerian (the case in the *Master-singers*)? Or that even married women are willingly saved by a cavalier (the case of *Isolde*)? Or that "the old God," after he has compromised himself morally in every respect, is finally saved by a freethinker and immoralist (the case in the *Nibelung's Ring*)? Admire especially this last profundity! Do you understand it? I take good care not to understand it . . . That other lessons also may be derived from these works, I would rather prove than deny. That one can be brought to despair by a Wagnerian ballet—*and* to virtue (once more the case of *Tannhäuser*)! That the worst consequences may result if one does not go to bed at the right time (once more the case of *Lohengrin*). That one should never know too exactly whom one marries (for the third time the case of *Lohengrin*).—*Tristan and Isolde* extols the perfect husband, who on a certain occasion has only one question in his mouth: "But why have you not told me that sooner? Nothing was simpler than that!" Answer:

> "In truth I cannot tell it.
> What thou dost ask
> Remains for aye unanswered."

Lohengrin contains a solemn proscription of investigation and questioning. Wagner, accordingly, advocates the Christian doctrine, "Thou shalt *believe,* and must *believe*" It is an offence against the highest and holiest to be scientific . . . The *Flying Dutchman* preaches the sublime doctrine that woman makes even the most vagabond person settle down, or, in Wagnerian language, "saves" him. Here we take the liberty to ask a question. Granted that it is true, would it at the same time be desirable? What becomes of the "Wandering Jew," adored and *settled down* by a woman? He simply ceases to be the eternal wanderer, he marries, and is of no more interest to us. Translated into actuality: the danger of artists, of geniuses—for these are the "Wandering Jews"—lies in woman: *adoring* women are their ruin. Hardly anyone has sufficient character to resist being corrupted—being "saved"—when he finds himself treated as a god: he forthwith *condescends* to woman.—Man is cowardly before all that is eternally feminine: women know it.—In many cases of feminine love (perhaps precisely in the most celebrated cases), love is only a more refined *parasitism,* a nestling in a strange soul, sometimes even in a strange body—Ah! at what expense always to "the host!"——

Goethe's fate in moralic-acid, old-maidenish Germany is known. He was always a scandal to the Germans; he has had honest admirers only among Jewesses. Schiller, "noble" Schiller, who blustered round their ears with high-flown phrases, *he* was according to their taste. Why did they reproach Goethe? For the "Mountain of Venus," and because he had composed Venetian epigrams. Klopstock had already preached to him on morals; there was a time when Herder had a preference for the word "Priapus," when speaking of Goethe. Even *Wilhelm Meister* was only regarded as a symptom of *décadence,* of "going to the dogs" in morals. The "menagerie of tame cattle" which it exhibits, and the "meanness" of the hero, exasperated Niebuhr, for example, who finally breaks out into a lamentation which *Biterolf*[2] might have chanted: "Hardly anything can produce a more painful impression than a great mind despoiling itself of its wings, and seeking its virtuosity in something far lower, *while it renounces the higher*" . . . The cultured maiden was however especially roused: all the little courts—every sort of "Wartburg" in Germany—crossed themselves before Goethe, before the "unclean spirit" in Goethe.—Wagner has set *this* history to music. He *saves* Goethe, that goes without saying, but he does it in such a way that he adroitly takes the part of the cultured maiden at the same time. Goethe is saved; a prayer saves him, a cultured maiden *draws him upward* . . .

What Goethe would have thought of Wagner? Goethe once proposed to himself the question, "What is the danger which hovers over all romanticists: the fate of the romanticist?" His answer was, "Suffocation by chewing moral and religious absurdities over again." In fewer words: *Parsifal*——The philosopher adds an epilogue to that answer. *Holiness*—the last of the higher values perhaps still seen by the populace and woman, the horizon of the ideal for all who are naturally myopic. For philosophers, however, it is like every other horizon, a mere misapprehension, a sort of door-closing of the region where their world only *commences—their* danger, *their* ideal, *their* desirability . . . Expressed more politely: *la philosophic ne suffit pas au grand nombre. Il lui faut la sainteté.*—

4

I further recount the story of the *Nibelung's Ring.* It belongs to this place. It is also a story of salvation, only, this time, it is Wagner himself who is saved. For the half of his life, Wagner has believed in *revolution,* as none but a Frenchman has ever believed in it. He sought for it in the Runic characters of myths, he believed that he found in Siegfried the typical revolutionist.—"Whence comes all the evil in the world?" Wagner asked himself. From "old conventions" he answered, like every revolutionary ideologist. That means from customs, laws, morals, and institutions, from all that the old world, old society rest on. "How does one get rid of the evil in the world? How does one do away with old society?" Only by declaring war against "conventions" (traditional usage and morality). *That is what Siegfried does.* He commences early with it, very early: his procreation already is a declaration of war against morality—he comes into the world through adultery and incest . . . It is *not* the legend, but Wagner who is the inventor of this radical trait; on this point he has *corrected* the legend . . . Siegfried continues as he commenced: he follows only the first impulse, he casts aside all tradition, all reverence, all *fear.* Whatever displeases him, he stabs down. He runs irreverently to the attack on the old Deities. His principal undertaking, however, is for the purpose of *emancipating woman*—"saving Brunnhilde" . . . Siegfried and Brunnhilde; the sacrament of free love;

---

[2] A personage in Wagner's *Tannhäuser.*

the dawn of the golden age; the twilight of the Gods of old morality!—*evil is done away with* . . . Wagner's vessel ran merrily on this course for a long time. Here, undoubtedly, Wagner sought *his* highest goal.—What happened? A misfortune. The vessel went on a reef; Wagner was run aground. The reef was Schopenhauer's philosophy; Wagner was run aground on a *contrary* view of things. What had he set to music? Optimism. Wagner was ashamed. In addition, it was an optimism for which Schopenhauer had formed a malicious epithet—*infamous* optimism. He was once more ashamed. He thought long over it; his situation seemed desperate . . . A way out of the difficulty finally dawned on his mind. The reef on which he was wrecked—how would it be if he interpreted it as the *goal,* the ultimate purpose, the real meaning of his voyage? To be wrecked *here*—that was a goal also. *Bene navigavi cum naufragium feci* . . . And he translated the *Nibelung's Ring* into Schopenhauerism. Everything goes wrong, everything goes to ruin, the new world is as bad as the old.—Nothingness, the Indian Circe, makes a sign . . . Brunnhilde, who according to the earlier design had to take leave with a song in honour of free love, solacing the world in anticipation of a Socialistic Utopia in which "all will be well," has now something else to do. She has first to study Schopenhauer; she has to put into verse the fourth book of the "World as Will and Representation." *Wagner was saved* . . . In "all seriousness, that *was* a salvation. The service for which Wagner is indebted to Schopenhauer is immense. It was only the *philosopher of décadence* who -enabled the artist of *décadence* to discover himself.

5

The *artist of décadence*—that is the word. And it is here that my seriousness commences. I am not at all inclined to be a quiet spectator, when this *décadent* ruins our health—and music along with it. Is Wagner a man at all? Is he not rather a disease? Everything he touches he makes morbid—*he has made music morbid.*—

A typical *décadent,* who feels himself necessary with his corrupt taste, who claims that it is a higher taste, who knows how to make his depravity be regarded as a law, as a progress, as fulfillment.

And nobody defends himself. Wagner's power of seduction becomes prodigious, the smoke of incense steams around him, the misunderstanding about him calls itself "Gospel"—it is by no means the *poor in spirit* exclusively whom he has convinced.

I should like to open the windows a little. Air! More air!—

It does not surprise me that people deceive themselves about Wagner in Germany. The contrary would surprise me. The Germans have created for themselves a Wagner whom they can worship; they were never psychologists, they are grateful by misunderstanding. But that people also deceive themselves about Wagner in Paris! where people are almost nothing else but psychologists. And in St. Petersburg! where things are still divined which are not divined even in Paris. How intimately related to the entire European *décadence* must Wagner be, when he is not recognised by it as a *décadent.* He belongs to it: he is its Protagonist, its greatest name . . . People honour themselves by exalting him to the skies.—For it is already a sign of *décadence* that no one defends himself against Wagner. Instinct is weakened. What should be shunned attracts people. What drives still faster into the abyss is put to the lips.—You want an example? One need only observe the *régime* which the anæmic, the gouty, and the diabetic prescribe for themselves. Definition of the vegetarian: a being who needs a strengthening diet. To recognize what is hurtful, as hurtful, *to be able* to deny one's self what is hurtful, is a sign of youth and vitality. The exhausted is *allured* by what is hurtful; the vegetarian by his pot-herbs. Disease itself may be a stimulus to life: only, a person must be sound enough for such a stimulus! Wagner increases exhaustion; it is *on that account* that he allures the weak and exhausted. Oh, the rattlesnake joy of the old master, when he always saw just "the little children" come to him!

I give prominence to this point of view: Wagner's art is morbid. The problems which he brings upon the stage,—nothing but problems of hysterics—the convulsiveness of his emotion, his over-excited sensibility, his taste, which always asked for stronger stimulants, his instability, which he disguised as principles, and, not least, the choice of his heroes and heroines, regarded as physiological types (a gallery of morbid individuals!): altogether these symptoms represent a picture of disease about which there can be no mistake. *Wagner est une névrose.* Nothing is perhaps better known at present, at any rate nothing is studied more than the Protean character of degeneracy, which here crystallises as art and artist. Our physicians and physiologists have in Wagner their most interesting case, at least a very complete case. Just because nothing is more modern than this entire morbidness, this decrepitude and over-excitability of the nervous mechanism, Wagner is the *modern artist par excellence,* the Cagliostro of modernism. In his art there is mixed, in the most seductive manner, the things at present most necessary for everybody—the three great stimulants of the exhausted, *brutality, artifice,* and *innocence* (idiocy).

Wagner is a great ruin for music. He has divined in music the expedient for exciting fatigued nerves—he has thus made music morbid. He possesses no small inventive ability in the art of pricking up once more the most exhausted, and calling back to life those who are half-dead. He is the master of hypnotic passes; he upsets, like the bulls, the very strongest. The *success* of Wagner—his success on the nerves, and consequently on women—has made all the ambitious musical world disciples of his magical art. And not the ambitious only, the *shrewd* also . . . At present money is only made by morbid music, our great theatres live by Wagner.

6

I again allow myself a little gaiety. I suppose the case that the *success* of Wagner became embodied, took form, and that, disguised as a philanthropic musical savant, it mixed among young artists. How do you think it would express itself under the circumstances?—

My friends, it would say, let us have five words among ourselves. It is easier to make bad music than good music. What if, apart from that, it were also more advantageous? more effective, more persuasive, more inspiriting, more sure? more *Wagnerian? Pulchrum est paucorum hominum.* Bad enough! We understand Latin, we perhaps also understand our advantage. The beautiful has its thorns; we are aware of that. What is the good, then, of beauty? Why not rather the grand, the sublime, the gigantic, that which moves the *masses?*—And once more: it is easier to be gigantic than to be beautiful; we are aware of that . . .

We know the masses, we know the theatre. The best that sit in it, German youths, horned Siegfrieds and other Wagnerians, require the sublime, the profound, the overpowering. Thus much we can accomplish. And the others that sit in the theatre—the culture-cretins, the little *blasés,* the eternally feminine, the good digesters, in short the *people*—similarly require the sublime, the profound, and the overpowering. Those have all one kind of logic. "He who upsets us is strong; he who raises us is divine; he who makes us imaginative is profound." Let us decide, Messrs. the musicians: let us upset them, let us raise them, let us make them imaginative. Thus much we can accomplish.

As regards the making imaginative, it is here that our conception of "style" has its starting point. Above all, there must be no thought! Nothing is more compromising than a thought! But the state of mind which *precedes* thought, the travail of yet unborn thoughts, the promise of future thoughts, the world as it was before God created it—a recrudescence of chaos . . . chaos makes imaginative . . .

In the language of the master: infinity, but without melody.

In the second place, as concerns the upsetting, it already belongs in part to physiology. Let us study first of all the instruments. Some of them persuade even the bowels (they *open* the doors, as Handel says), others charm the spinal marrow. The colour of sound is decisive here; *what* resounds is almost indifferent. Let us refine on *this* point! What is the use of wasting ourselves on other matters? Let us be characteristic in sound, even to foolishness! It is attributed to our genius when we give much to conjecture in our sounds! Let us irritate the nerves, let us strike them dead, let us make use of lightning and thunder,—that upsets . . .

Above all, however, *passion* upsets.—Let there be no misunderstanding among us with regard to passion. Nothing is less expensive than passion. One can dispense with all the virtues of counterpoint, one need not have learned anything,—one can always use passion. Beauty is difficult: let us guard ourselves against beauty! . . . And *melody* still more! Let us disparage, my friends, let us disparage, if we are serious about the ideal, let us disparage melody! Nothing is more dangerous than a fine melody! Nothing more certainly ruins the taste. We are lost, my friends, if fine melodies are again loved! . . .

Principle: Melody is immoral. *Proof:* Palestrina. *Application:* Parsifal. The want of melody even sanctifies . . .

And this is the definition of passion. Passion—or the gymnastics of the loathsome on the rope of enharmonics.—Let us dare, my friends, to be loathsome! Wagner has dared it! Let us splash before us, undismayed, the mire of the most odious harmonies! Let us not spare our hands! It is thus only that we become *natural* . . .

At last counsel! Perhaps it embraces all in one:—*Let us be idealists!* If this is not the most expedient thing we can do, it is at least the wisest. In order to raise men, we ourselves must be exalted. Let us walk above the clouds, let us harangue the infinite, let us surround ourselves with grand symbols! *Sursum! Bumbum!*—there is no better counsel. Let "fullness of heart" be our argument; let "fine feeling" be our advocate. Virtue still wins the case against counterpoint. "He who makes us better—how could it be that he was not good himself?" such has always been the conclusion of mankind. Let us therefore make mankind better!—one thereby becomes good (one thereby becomes "classic" even: Schiller became a "classic"). Seeking after ignoble sense-excitement, after so-called beauty, has enervated the Italians; let us remain German! Even Mozart's relation to music—Wagner has told *us* by way of consolation!—was frivolous after all . . . Let us never admit that music "serves for recreation," that it "cheers up," that it "furnishes enjoyment." *Let us never furnish enjoyment!*—we are lost, if people again think of art as hedonistic . . . That belongs to the bad eighteenth century . . . On the other hand, nothing might be more advisable (we say it apart) than a dose of—*hypocrisy, sit venia verbo.* That gives dignity.—And let us choose the hour when it is suitable to look black, to sigh publicly, to sigh in a Christian manner, to exhibit large Christian sympathy. "Man is depraved: who will save him? *What will save him?*" Let us not answer. Let us be careful.

Let us struggle against our ambition, which would like to found religions. But nobody must venture to doubt that *we* save him, that *our* music alone brings salvation . . . (Wagner's Essay, "Religion and Art").

7

Enough! Enough! I fear sinister reality will have been too plainly recognised under my cheerful lines—the picture of a decline in art, of a decline also in the artists. The latter, a decline of character, would perhaps receive a provisory expression with this formula: the musician is now becoming a stage-player, his art is developing more and more into a talent for *lying.* I shall have an opportunity (in a chapter of my principal work, which bears the title, "A Physiology of Art") of showing in detail how this total transformation of art into stage-playing is just as definite an expression of physiological degeneration (more exactly, a form of hysterics) as any of the corruptions and weaknesses of the art inaugurated by Wagner; for example, the restlessness of its optics, which necessitates continual changing of posture before it. One understands nothing of Wagner so long as one only sees in him a sport of nature, a caprice, a whim, or an accident. He was no "defective," "abortive," or "contradictory" genius, as has occasionally been said. Wagner was something *complete,* a typical *décadent,* in whom all "free will" was lacking, all whose characteristics were determined by necessity. If anything is interesting in Wagner, it is the logic with which a physiological trouble, as practice and procedure, as innovation in principles and crisis in taste, advances step by step, from conclusion to conclusion.

I confine myself this time solely to the question of *style.*—What is the characteristic of all *literary décadence?* It is that the life no longer resides in the whole. The word gets the upper hand and jumps out of the sentence, the sentence stretches too far and obscures the meaning of the page, the page acquires life at the expense of the whole—the whole is no longer a whole. But that is the simile for every style of *décadence:* always anarchy of the atoms, disgregation of will, in the language of morality, "liberty of the individual,"— widened to a political theory, "*equal* rights for all." Life, *equal* vitality, vibration and exuberance of life pushed back into the most minute structures, the others *poor* in life. Everywhere paralysis, distress, and torpor, *or* hostility and chaos, always becoming more striking, as one ascends to ever higher forms of organisation. The whole has ceased to live altogether; it is composite, summed up, artificial, an unnatural product.

There is hallucination at the commencement in Wagner—not of tones, but of gestures; for these he seeks the appropriate semeiotic tones. If you want to admire him, see him at work here: how he separates, how he arrives at little unities, how he animates them, inflates them, and renders them visible. But by so doing his power exhausts itself: the rest is worth nothing. How pitiable, how confused, how laic is his mode of "developing," his attempt to piece at least into one another, things which have not grown out of one another! His manner here reminds one of the *Frères de Goncourt,* whose style approaches Wagner's in other respects also. A sort of pity is aroused for so much trouble. That Wagner has masked under the guise of a principle his incapacity for creating organically, that he asserts a "dramatic style" where we assert merely his incapacity for any style, corresponds to an audacious habit which has accompanied Wagner all his life: he posits a principle where he lacks a faculty (very different in this respect, let us say in passing, from old Kant, who loved *another* kind of audacity: whenever he lacked a principle, he posited a "faculty" in human beings . . .). Once more let it be said that

Wagner is only worthy of admiration and love in the invention of *minutiæ,* in the elaboration of details;—here we have every right to proclaim him as a master of the first rank, as our greatest *miniaturist* in music, who compresses into the smallest space an infinitude of meaning and sweetness. His wealth of colours, of demi-tints, of the mysteries of vanishing light, spoils us to such a degree that almost all other musicians seem too robust afterwards.—If you will believe me, the highest conception of Wagner is not to be got from what at present pleases in his works. That has been invented to persuade the masses; one of our class bounds back in presence of it, as before an all too impudent fresco. What do *we* care for the *agaçante* brutality of the Overture of *Tannhäuser?* or for the Circus of the *Walkyrie?* Whatever has become popular in Wagner's music apart from the theatre is of a doubtful flavour and spoils the taste. The *Tannhäuser* March seems to me to raise a suspicion of Philistinism; the Overture of the *Flying Dutchman* is much ado about nothing; the Prelude to *Lohengrin* gave the first example, only too insidious, only too successful, of how one may hypnotise with music (I dislike all music that has no higher ambition than to persuade the nerves). A part, however, from Wagner the magnetiser and fresco-painter, there is yet a Wagner who deposits J little jewels in his works, our greatest melancholist in music, full of flashes, delicacies, and words of comfort (in which no one has anticipated him, the master of the tones of a melancholy and comatose happiness . . . A lexicon of the most familiar language of Wagner, nothing but short phrases of from five to fifteen measures, nothing but music which *nobody knows* . . . Wagner had the virtue of the *décadents,* pity . . .

8

—"Very good! But how can one lose one's taste for this *décadent,* if one is not perchance a musician, if one is not perchance a *décadent* one's self?"—Reversely! How is it we *can't* do it? Just attempt it! You are not aware who Wagner is; he is quite a great stage-player! Does there at all exist a more profound, a more *oppressive* effect in the theatre? Do look at these youths—benumbed, pale, and breathless! They are Wagnerians, they understand nothing of music—and nevertheless Wagner becomes master over them . . . Wagner's art presses with the weight of a hundred atmospheres: bow yourselves just, it is unavoidable . . . Wagner the stage-player is a tyrant, his pathos overthrows every kind of taste, every kind of resistance.—Who has such convincing power of attitude, who sees the attitude so definitely before everything else? This holding the breath of Wagnerian pathos, this unwillingness to let an extreme feeling escape, this dread-inspiring *duration* of conditions where momentary suspense is enough to choke one!——

Was Wagner a musician at all? At least he was something else in a *higher degree,* namely, an incomparable *histrio,* the greatest mime, the most astonishing theatrical genius that the Germans have had, our *scenic artist par excellence.* His place is elsewhere than in the history of music, with the grand true geniuses of which he must not be confounded. Wagner *and* Beethoven—that is a blasphemy—and in the end an injustice even to Wagner . . . He was also as a musician only that which he was in other respects: he *became* a musician, he *became* a poet, because the tyrant in him, his stage-player genius, compelled him to it. One finds out nothing about Wagner as long as one has not found out his dominating instinct.

Wagner was *not* a musician by instinct. He proved this himself by abandoning all lawfulness, and—to speak more definitely—all style in music, in order to make out of it what he required, a theatrical rhetoric, a means for expression, for strengthening attitudes, for suggestion, for the psychologically picturesque. Wagner might here pass for an inventor and an innovator of the first rank—*he has immeasurably increased the speaking power of music;* he is the Victor Hugo of music as language! Provided always one grants that music *may,* under certain conditions, not be music, but speech, tool, or *ancilla dramaturgica.* Wagner's music, *not* taken under protection by theatrical taste, a very tolerant taste, is simply bad music, perhaps the worst that has ever been made. When a musician can no longer count three, he becomes "dramatic," he becomes "Wagnerian" . . .

Wagner has almost discovered what magic can be wrought with a music decomposed and reduced, as it were, to the *elementary.* His consciousness of it goes so far as to be disquieting, like his instinct for finding a higher lawfulness and a *style* unnecessary. The elementary *suffices*—sound, movement, colour, in short, the sensuality of music. Wagner never calculates as a musician from any kind of musical conscience; he wants effect, he wants nothing but effect. And he knows that on which he has to operate! He has, in this respect, the unscrupulousness which Schiller possessed, which everyone possesses who is connected with the stage; he has also Schiller's contempt for the world, which has to sit at his feet. A person is a stage-player in virtue of having a certain discernment in advance of other men, viz., that what has to operate as true must not be true at all. The proposition has been formulated by Talma: it contains the entire psychology of the stage-player, it contains—let us not doubt it—his morality also. Wagner's music is never true.

—But *it is taken as true,* and so it is all right.—As long as people continue childish, and Wagnerian in addition, they think of Wagner even as rich, as a paragon of lavishness, as a great landed proprietor in the empire of sound. They admire in him what young French people admire in Victor Hugo, the "royal generosity." Later on people admire both of them for the very reverse reasons: as masters and models of economy, as *prudent* amphitryons. Nobody equals them in the ability to present an apparently princely table at a modest cost.—The Wagnerian, with his devout stomach, becomes satiated even with the fare which his master conjures up for him. We others, however, who, alike in books and in music, want *substance* more than anything else, and for whom merely "represented" feasts hardly suffice, we are much worse off. Speaking plainly, Wagner does not give us enough to chew. His *recitativo*—little meat, somewhat more bone, and very much sauce—has been christened by me *"Alla genovese;"* wherewith I certainly do not mean to flatter the Genoese, but rather the *older recitativo,* the *recitativo secco.* As for the Wagnerian "leading motive," I lack all culinary intelligence for it. If I were pressed, I would perhaps assign to it the value of an ideal toothpick, as an occasion for dispensing with the *rest* of the food. The "arias" of Wagner are still left.—And now I do not say a word more.

9

In sketching dramatic action, likewise, Wagner is above all a stage-player. That which first suggests itself to him is a scene with an absolutely sure effect, a veritable *actio*,[3] with a *haut-relief* of gesture, a scene which *upsets;*—he thinks this out thoroughly, it is only out of this that he derives his characters. All the rest follows therefrom in accordance with a technical economy which has no reasons to be subtle. It is not the public of Corneille Wagner has to indulge; it is merely the nineteenth century. Wagner would decide with regard to the "one thing needful" in much the same manner as every other stage-player decides now-a-days: a series of strong scenes, each stronger than the other,—and much *sage* stupidity in between. He seeks first of all to guarantee to himself the effect of his work; he begins with the third act, he *tests* for himself his work by its final effect. With such a theatrical talent for guide, one is in no danger of creating a drama unawares. A drama requires *hard* logic: but what did Wagner ever care about logic! Let us repeat: it was *not* the public of Corneille he had to indulge, it was mere Germans! One knows the technical problem in solving which the dramatist applies all his power and often sweats blood: to give *necessity* to the plot, and likewise to the *dénouement,* so that both are possible only in one way, so that both give the impression of freedom (principle of the least expenditure of force). Now Wagner sweats the least blood here; it is certain that he makes the least expenditure of force on plot and *dénouement.* You may put any one of Wagner's "plots" under the microscope;—I promise you will have to laugh at what you see. Nothing more enlivening than the plot of *Tristan,* unless it be that of the *Master-singers.* Wagner is *not* a dramatist; let us not be imposed upon! He loved the word "drama;" that was all—he always loved fancy words. The word "drama," in his writings, is nevertheless purely a misunderstanding (*and* shrewd policy: Wagner always affected superiority toward the word "opera"), much in the same manner as the word "spirit" in the New Testament is purely a misunderstanding.—From the first, he was not enough of a psychologist for the drama; he avoided instinctively psychological motivation. By what means? By always putting idiosyncrasy in its place . . . Very modern, is it not? very Parisian! very *décadent!* . . . The *plots,* let us say in passing, which Wagner really knows how to work out by means of dramatic invention, are of quite another kind. I give an example. Let us take the case of Wagner requiring a woman's voice. An entire act *without* a woman's voice—that does not do! But for the moment none of the "heroines" are free. What does Wagner do!. He emancipates the oldest woman in the world, Erda. "Up! old grandmother! You have got to sing!" Erda sings. Wagner's purpose is served. He immediately discharges the old dame again. "Why really did you come? Retire! Please go to sleep again!"—*In summa: a* scene full of mythological horrors, which makes the Wagnerians *imaginative . . .*

—"But the *contents* of the Wagnerian texts! their mythical contents, their eternal contents!"—Question: how does one test these contents, these eternal contents! The

---

[3] NOTE.—It has been a veritable misfortune for Æsthetics that the word "drama" has always been translated by "action." Wagner is not the only one who errs here; all the world is still in error about the matter; even the philologists, who ought to know better. The ancient drama had grand *pathetic scenes* in view,—it just excluded action (relegated it *previous to* the commencement, or *behind* the scene). The word "drama" is of Doric origin, and according to Dorian usage signifies "event," "history," both words in a hieratic sense. The oldest drama represented local legend, the "sacred history" on which the establishment of the cult rested (consequently no doing, but a happening: δρᾶν in Dorian does not at all signify "to do").

chemist gives the reply: one translates Wagner into the real, into the modern—let us be still more cruel,—into civil life! What then becomes of Wagner! To speak in confidence, I have attempted it. Nothing more entertaining, nothing more recommendable for pleasure walks, than to recount Wagner to one's self in *more modern* proportions: for example, *Parsifal* as a candidate in divinity, with a public school education (the latter indispensable for *pure folly*[4]). What *surprises* one then experiences! Would you believe it that the Wagnerian heroines, each and all, when one has only stripped them of their heroic trappings, are like counterparts of *Madame Bovary!*—And how one comprehends, inversely, that Flaubert *was at liberty* to translate his heroine into Scandinavian, or Carthaginian, and then to offer her, mythologised, to Wagner as a libretto. Yes, taken as a whole, Wagner appears to have had no interest in any other problems than those which at present interest petty Parisian *décadents*. Always just five steps from the hospital! Nothing but quite modern problems, nothing but problems of *a great city!* don't you doubt it! . . . Have you remarked (it belongs to this association of ideas) that the Wagnerian heroines have no children? They *cannot* have children . . . The despair with which Wagner has dealt with the problem of permitting Siegfried to be born at all, reveals *how* modern his sentiments were on this point.—Siegfried "emancipates woman"—but without hope of posterity.—Finally, a fact which perplexes us: Parsifal is the father of Lohengrin! How has he done that?—Have we here to recollect that "chastity works *miracles?*" . . .

Wagnerus dixit princeps in castitate auctoritas.

10

A word yet, in passing, concerning Wagner's writings: they are, among other things, a school of *expediency*. The system of procedure which Wagner uses is to be employed in a hundred other cases,—he that hath an ear, let him hear. Perhaps I shall have a claim to public gratitude, if I give precise expression to his three most valuable principles of procedure:—

Whatever Wagner *cannot* accomplish is objectionable.

Wagner might accomplish much more, but he is unwilling—owing to strictness of principle.

Whatever Wagner *can* accomplish, no one will imitate, no one has anticipated, no one *ought* to imitate . . . Wagner is divine . . .

These three propositions are the quintessence of Wagner's writings: the rest is— "literature."

—Not all the music up till now has had need of literature: one does well here to seek for a satisfactory reason. Is it that Wagner's music is too difficult to understand? Or did he fear the contrary, that it would be understood too easily, that it would *not be difficult enough* to understand?—In fact, he has all his life repeated one phrase: that his music does not simply mean music! But more! Infinitely more! . . . "*Not simply* music"—no musician speaks in such a manner! Let it be said once more, Wagner was unable to cut out of the block; he had no choice at all, he was obliged to make patch-work—"motives," attitudes, formulæ, reduplications, centuplications; as a musician he remained a rhetorician:—on that account he *was compelled* as a matter of principle to bring the device, "It implies," into the foreground. "Music is always just a means;" that was his

---

[4] Nietzsche here refers to the etymology of Parsifal (pure fool) which Wagner adopted.

theory, that was the only *praxis* at all possible for him. But no musician thinks in such a way.—Wagner had need of literature in order to persuade all the world to take his music seriously, to take it as profound, "because it *meant* Infinity;" all his life he was the commentator of the "Idea."—What does Elsa signify? There is no doubt however: Elsa is "the unconscious *spirit of the people*" ("with this idea I necessarily developed to a complete revolutionist").[5]

Let us recollect that Wagner was young when Hegel and Schelling led men's minds astray; that he found out, that he grasped firmly what only a German takes seriously—"the Idea," that is to say, something obscure, uncertain, mysterious; that among Germans clearness is an objection, and logic is disproof. Schopenhauer has, with severity, accused the epoch of Hegel and Schelling of dishonesty—with severity, and also with injustice: he himself, the old pessimistic false-coiner, has in no way acted "more honestly" than his more celebrated contemporaries. Let us leave morality out of the game: Hegel is a *flavour* . . . And not only a German, but a European flavour!—A flavour which Wagner understood!—which he felt himself equal to!—which he has immortalised!—He merely made application of it to music—he invented for himself a style which "meant Infinity"—he became the *heir of Hegel* . . . Music as "Idea"——

And how Wagner was understood! The same sort of men who were enthusiastic for Hegel, are at present enthusiastic for Wagner: in his school Hegelian is even *written!*—Above all, the German youth understood him. The two words, "infinite" and "significance," quite sufficed; he enjoyed an incomparable pleasure in hearing them. It is *not* with music that Wagner has won the youth over to himself, it is with the "Idea:"—it is the mysteriousness of his art, its game of hide-and-seek among a hundred symbols, its polychromy of the ideal, which has led and allured these youths to Wagner! it is Wagner's genius for forming clouds, his gripping, sweeping and roving through the air, his ubiquity and nullibiety—precisely the same proceeding with which once Hegel misled and seduced the youth! In the midst of Wagner's multiplicity, fullness, and arbitrariness, they are justified, as it were, in their own eyes—they are "saved."—They hear with trembling how in his art the *sublime symbols* become audible with gentle thunder out of the cloudy distance; they are not out of temper if the atmosphere here sometimes becomes grey, frightful, and cold. For they are each and all related to bad weather, German weather, like Wagner himself! Woden is their God: Woden, however, is the God of bad weather . . . They are right, these German youths, such as they are: how could they miss in Wagner what we others, we *Halcyonians,* miss in him:—*la gaya scienza;* light feet; wit, fire, grace, lofty logic; the dance of the stars, haughty intellectuality; the tremor of southern light; the *smooth* sea—perfection . . .

11

—I have explained where Wagner belongs to—*not* to the history of music. Nevertheless, what is his import for the history of music? *The advent of the stage-player in music:* a momentous event, which gives occasion to reflect, perhaps also to fear. In a formula, "Wagner and Liszt."—Never has the uprightness of musicians, their "genuineness," been put to such a dangerous test. It is easily enough understood: great success, the success with the masses, is no longer on the side of genuineness,—one has to be a stage-player in order to obtain it!—Victor Hugo and Richard Wagner—they imply

---

[5] Quotations from Wagner.

one and the same truth, that in declining civilisations, wherever the arbitrating power falls into the hands of the masses, genuineness becomes superfluous, disadvantageous, and a drawback. It is only the stage-player that still awakens *great* enthusiasm.—Thus dawns the *golden age* for the stage-player—for him and all that is related to his species. Wagner marches with drums and fifes at the head of all the artists of elocution, of display, of virtuosity; he has first convinced the leaders of the orchestras, the machinists, and theatrical singers. Not to forget the musicians of the orchestra:—he "saved" them from tedium . . . The movement which Wagner created encroaches even on the domain of knowledge; entire sciences belonging thereto emerge slowly out of a scholasticism which is centuries old. To give an example, I call special attention to the service which *Riemann* has rendered to rhythmics; he is the first who has made current the essential idea of punctuation in music (it is a pity that by means of an ugly word he calls it "phrasing").— All these, I say it with gratitude, are the best, the most worthy of regard, among the worshippers of Wagner—they are simply right to worship Wagner. The same instinct unites them with one another, they see in him their highest type, they feel themselves transformed and elevated to power, even to great power, ever since he inflamed them with his peculiar ardour. Here indeed, if anywhere, the influence of Wagner has really been *beneficent.* In this sphere, there has never been so much thought, so much purpose, so much work. Wagner has inspired all these artists with a new conscience: what they at present require of themselves, what they *obtain* from themselves, they have never required before Wagner's time—formerly they were too modest for that. A different spirit rules in the theatre since the spirit of Wagner began to rule there: the most difficult is demanded, there is severe blaming, there is rarely praising,—the good, the excellent, is regarded as the rule. Taste is no longer necessary; not even voice. Wagner is only sung with a ruined voice: that has a "dramatic" effect. Even talent is excluded. The *espressivo* at any price, such as is demanded by the Wagnerian ideal, the *décadence* ideal, gets along badly with talent. *Virtue* only is the proper thing here—that is to say, drilling, automatism, "self-denial." Neither taste, nor voice, nor talent: there is only one thing needful for Wagner's stage—*Germanics!* . . . Definition of Germanics: obedience and long legs . . . It is full of deep significance that the advent of Wagner coincides with the advent of the "Empire;" both facts furnish proof of one and the same thing—obedience and long legs.—There has never been better obedience; there has never been better commanding. The Wagnerian musical directors, in particular, are worthy of an age which posterity will one day designate with timorous reverence, *the classical age of war.* Wagner understood how to command; by that means he was the great teacher also. He commanded as the inexorable will to himself, as the life-long discipline of himself: Wagner, who perhaps furnishes the most striking example of self-tyranny which the history of art supplies (even Alfieri, otherwise most nearly related to him, has been surpassed.—Remark of a Turinese).

12

By means of this insight that our stage-players are more worthy of adoration than ever, their dangerousness has not been conceived as less . . . But who yet doubts *what* I am after—what are the *three demands* for which my resentment, my solicitude, and my love for art, have at present opened my mouth?—

> *That the theatre may not become the master of art.*
> *That the stage-player may not become the corrupter of the genuine ones.*
> *That music may not become an art of lying.*

Friedrich Nietzsche.

POSTSCRIPT

The gravity of the last words permits me in this place to communicate in addition some passages from an unprinted dissertation, which at least leave no doubt concerning my seriousness in this matter. The dissertation is entitled, *What Wagner costs us.*

The adherence to Wagner costs dear. An obscure consciousness of this still exists at present. Even Wagner's success, his *triumph,* did not outroot this feeling radically. But formerly it was strong, it was formidable, it was like a gloomy hatred—throughout almost three-fourths of Wagner's lifetime. That resistance which he encountered among us Germans, cannot be estimated highly enough, nor sufficiently honoured. We defended ourselves against him as against a disease—*not* with arguments—one does not refute a disease,—but with obstruction, with mistrust, with aversion, with loathing, with a sullen seriousness, as if a great danger prowled around us in him. The aesthetic gentlemen compromised themselves when, out of three schools of German philosophy, they made an absurd attack upon Wagner's principles with "if" and "for"—what did he care for principles, even his own! The Germans, however, have had enough of reason in their instincts to prohibit themselves every "if" and "for" in this matter. An instinct is weakened when it is rationalised; for *by* rationalising itself it weakens itself. If there are indications that, in spite of the totality of European *décadence,* there yet resides in the German character a degree of healthfulness, an instinctive scent for what is injurious and threatens danger. I should like least of all to see this stolid resistance to Wagner undervalued among us. It does honour to us, it permits us even to hope: France could no longer dispense with so much healthfulness. The Germans, the *retarders par excellence* in history, are at present the most backward among the civilised peoples of Europe: this has its advantage,—they are thus relatively they *youngest.*

The adherence to Wagner costs dear. The Germans have only quite lately unlearned a sort of dread of him—the desire to *get rid of him* came upon them on every occasion.[6]—Do you recollect a curious occurrence, in which, just at the end, that old

---

[6] NOTE.—Was Wagner German at all? We have some reasons for asking this. It is difficult to discover in him any German trait whatsoever. Being a great learner, he has learned to imitate much that is German—that is all. His character itself is *in opposition* to what has hitherto been regarded as German—not to speak of the German musician!—His father was a stage-player named Geyer. A Geyer is almost an Adler* . . . What has hitherto been put in circulation as the "Life of Wagner" is *fable convenue,* if not worse. I confess my distrust of every point which rests solely on the testimony of Wagner himself. He had not pride enough for any truth whatsoever about himself, nobody was less proud; he remained, just like Victor Hugo, true to himself even in

feeling again, quite unexpectedly, made its appearance? It happened at the funeral of Wagner that the first Wagner Society in Germany, that of Munich, deposited on his tomb a wreath, the *inscription* on which immediately became celebrated. "Salvation to the Saviour!"—was how it read. Everybody admired the sublime inspiration which had dictated this inscription, everybody admired a taste in which the partisans of Wagner have a privilege; but many also (it was singular enough!) made the same little correction in the inscription: "Salvation *from* the Saviour!"—People recovered breath.—

The adherence to Wagner costs dear. Let us measure it in its effect upon civilisation. Whom has his movement really brought into the foreground? What has it more and more reared into magnitude?—More than anything else, the arrogance of the layman, of the idiotic art-amateur. He organises societies just now, he wants to make his "taste" prevail, he would like even to become the judge *in rebus musicis et musicantibus.* In the second place, an ever greater indifference to all severe, noble, conscientious training in the service of art; the belief in genius substituted, for it; in plain words, insolent dilettanteism (the formula for it is to be found in the *Master-singers*). In the third place, and worst of all, *Theatrocracy;*—absurdity of a belief in *precedence* of the theatre, in the right of *sovereignty* of the theatre over the arts, over art . . . But one has to tell the Wagnerians a hundred times to their face *what* the theatre is:—always just something *in subterposition* to art, always something merely secondary, something vulgarised, something suitably adapted for the masses, suitably falsified for them. Even Wagner has changed nothing of that: Bayreuth is big opera—but never *good* opera . . . The theatre is a form of demolatry in matters of taste, the theatre is an insurrection of the masses, a plébiscite *against* good taste. *The case of Wagner just proves this:* he gained the multitude,—he depraved the taste, he depraved even our taste for the opera!—

The adherence to Wagner costs dear. What does it make of the mind? *Does Wagner free the mind?*—He is possessed of every ambiguity, every equivocation, everything, in fact, which persuades the undecided, without making them conscious *what* they are persuaded to. Wagner is thereby a seducer in the grand style. There is nothing fatigued, nothing decrepit, nothing dangerous to life and derogatory to the world in spiritual matters, which would not be secretly taken under protection by his art,—it is the blackest obscurantism which he conceals in the luminous husks of the ideal. He flatters every nihilistic (Buddhistic) instinct and disguises it in music, he flatters every kind of Christianity, and every religious form of expression of *décadence.* Let us open our ears: everything that has grown up on the soil of *impoverished* life, the entire false coinage of transcendence and another world, has in Wagner's art its sublimest advocate—*not* in formulae (Wagner is too prudent to use formulae) but in its persuasion of sensuality, which, in its turn, again makes the mind tender and fatigued. Music as Circe . . . His last work is in this respect his greatest masterpiece. *Parsifal* will always maintain the chief place in the art of seduction, as its *stroke of genius* . . . I admire that work, I should like to have composed it myself; not having done so, *I at least understand it* . . . Wagner was never better inspired than at the end. The exquisiteness in the alliance of beauty and disease is here carried so far that it casts, as it were, a shadow over Wagner's earlier art:—it appears too bright, too healthy. Do you understand that? Health and brightness acting as a shadow? as an *objection* almost? . . . We are so far *pure fools* already . . . Never was there a greater connoisseur of musty, hieratic perfumes,—there never lived

---

biographical matters,—he remained a stage-player.
 *Geyer (vulture) and Adler (eagle) are both names of Jewish families.

such an expert in the knowledge of all the *little* infinite, of all the tremulous and exuberant, of all the femininism in the thesaurus of happiness!—Just drink, my friends, the philtres of this art! You nowhere find a more pleasant mode of enervating your mind, of forgetting your manliness under a rose-bush . . . Ah! this old magician! This Klingsor of all the Klingsors! How he makes war against *us* there with! against us, the free spirits! How he humours every cowardice of modern soul with Siren tones!—There was never such a *mortal hatred* of knowledge!—One here requires to be a Cynic to escape being seduced; one requires to be able to bite to avoid worshipping. Well! old seducer! The Cynic warns thee—*cave canem* . . .

The adherence to Wagner costs dear. I observe the youths who have long been exposed to his infection. The proximate effect, relatively innocent, relates to taste. Wagner's influence is like a continuous use of alcohol. It dulls, it obstructs the stomach with phlegm. Specific effect: degeneracy of the sense of rhythm. The Wagnerian at last comes to call rhythmical, what I myself, borrowing a Greek proverb, call "agitating the swamp." The corruption of the conceptions is undoubtedly much more dangerous. The youth becomes a moon-calf—an "idealist." He has got beyond science, in that respect he stands at the height of the master. On the other hand, he plays the philosopher; he writes Bayreuth journals; he solves all problems in the name of the Father, the Son, and the Holy Master. The most disquieting thing, to be sure, is the ruin of the nerves. You may go at night through any of the larger cities, and everywhere you hear instruments violated with solemn fury—a savage howling mingling therewith. What is taking place?—the youths are worshipping Wagner . . . Bayreuth rhymes itself with hydropathic-establishment.—A typical telegram from Bayreuth: *Bereits bereut* (rued already).—Wagner is bad for youths; he is fatal to women. What, in medical language, is a Wagnerienne?—It seems to me that a physician could not put this conscience-alternative with too much seriousness to brides: *either* the one *or* the other.—But they have already made their choice. One cannot serve two masters if one of them is called Wagner. Wagner has saved woman, therefore woman has built Bayreuth for him. Entire sacrifice, entire devotion, they have nothing they would not give him. Woman impoverishes herself in favour of the master, she becomes touching, she stands naked before him.—The Wagnerienne—the most gracious equivocalness to be found at present: she *embodies* Wagner's cause—in her sign, his cause *triumphs* . . . Ah, this old robber! He plunders us of our youths, he takes even our women as plunder, and drags them into his cavern . . . Ah, this old Minotaur! What he has already cost us! Every year trains of the finest maidens and youths are led into his labyrinth, that he may devour them,—every year all Europe strikes up the cry: "Off to Crete! Off to Crete!" . . .

SECOND POSTSCRIPT

My letter, it appears, is liable to a misapprehension. On certain countenances the indications of gratitude show themselves; I hear even a discreet mirth. I should prefer here, as in many things, to be understood.—But since a new animal ravages in the vineyards of German intellect, the Empire worm, celebrated *Rhinoxera,* nothing I say is any longer understood. The *Kreuzzeitung* itself attests this to me, not to speak of the *Literarisches Centralblatt.*—I have given to the Germans the profoundest books they at all possess—a sufficient reason why they should not understand a word of them . . . If in *this* work I make an attack on Wagner—and incidentally on a German "taste,"—if I have hard words for the Bayreuth cretinism, I should like least of all to make an entertainment there with for any *other* musicians. *Other* musicians do not come into consideration in presence of Wagner. Things are bad everywhere. The decay is universal. The disease is deep seated. If Wagner's name typifies the *ruin of musky* as Bernini's name typifies the ruin of sculpture, he is not by any means its cause. He has only accelerated its *tempo,*—to be sure, in such a way that one stands frightened before the almost instantaneous descent, downwards, into the abyss. He had the *naïveté* of *décadence:* that was his superiority. He believed in it, he did not stop before any logic of *décadence.* The others *hesitate*—that distinguishes them. Nothing else! . . . That which Wagner and the "others" have in common—I enumerate it: the decline of organising power; the abuse of traditional means without the *justifying* capacity, that of attaining the end; the false coinage in the imitation of great forms, for which at present nobody is sufficiently strong, sufficiently proud, sufficiently self-confident, or sufficiently *healthy;* the over-liveliness of the smallest details; emotion at any price; refinement as the expression of *impoverished* life; always more nerves in place of flesh.—I know only one musician who is at present still in a position to cut an overture out of the block, and nobody knows him[7] . . . What is at present famous does not create "better" music in comparison with Wagner's, but only music which is more indecisive, more indifferent:—more indifferent, because the incomplete is set aside *by the presence of the complete.* Wagner was complete; but he was complete corruption; he was courage, he was will, he was *conviction* in corruption— of what import, then, is Johannes Brahms! . . . His good fortune was a German misapprehension: he was taken for Wagner's antagonist,—an antagonist to Wagner was *needed!*—That does not produce *indispensable* music, it produces in the first instance too much music!—If you are not rich, be proud enough for poverty! . . . The sympathy which Brahms here and there undeniably inspires, apart altogether from such party interest and party misunderstanding, was for a long time an enigma to me, until finally, almost by accident, I came to perceive that he operated on a certain type of persons. He has the melancholy of impotency; he does *not* create out of plenitude, he is thirsty for plenitude. If one deducts his imitations, what he borrows either from the great ancient or the exotic modern forms of style—he is a master in the art of copying,—there remains, as his most striking peculiarity, the *longing mood . . .* That is divined by all who long, by all who are dissatisfied. He is too little of a person, too little centralised. . . . That is what the "impersonal," the peripheristic understand,—they love him on that account. He is especially the musician of a class of unsatisfied ladies. Fifty paces further on we find the Wagnerienne—just as we find Wagner fifty paces further on than Brahms,—the Wagnerienne, a better stamped, more interesting, and, above all, a *more gracious* type. Brahms is moving, as long as he is in secret reveries, or mourns over himself—in that he is "modern;" he becomes cold, he is of no more interest to us, immediately that he *becomes the heir* of the classics . . . One likes to speak of Brahms as the *heir* of Beethoven: I know of no more considerate euphemism.—All that at present makes pretensions to the "grand style" in music is thereby *either* false with respect to us, *or* false with respect to itself. This alternative is sufficiently thought-worthy, for it involves a casuistry with regard to the worth of the two cases. "False with respect to *us:*" the instinct of most people protests against that—they do not want to be deceived; though I myself, to be sure, should still prefer this type to the other ("false with respect to *itself*"). This is *my* taste.—Expressed more simply for the "poor in spirit:" Brahms—*or* Wagner . . . Brahms is *no* stage-player.—One may subsume a good many of the *other* musicians under the

---

[7] It is Peter Gast, a disciple and friend of Nietzsche's, who is here referred to.

conception of Brahms.—I do not say a word of the sagacious apes of Wagner, for example, of Goldmark: with his *Queen of Sheba* one belongs to the menagerie—one may exhibit one's self.—What can be done well at present, what can be done in a masterly manner, is only the small things. It is here only that honesty is still possible.—Nothing, however, can cure music *in* the main thing, *of* the main thing, of the fatality of being the expression of a physiological contradiction,—of being *modern.* The best instruction, the most conscientious schooling, the most thorough intimacy with the old masters, yea, even isolation in their society—all that is only palliative, or, speaking more strictly, *illusory;* because one has no longer the physical capacity which is presupposed: be it that of the strong race of a Handel, be it the overflowing animality of a Rossini.—Not everyone has the *right* to every teacher: that is true of whole epochs.—The possibility is not in itself excluded that there still exist, somewhere in Europe, *remains* of stronger races, men typically inopportune: from thence a *delayed* beauty and perfection even for music might still be hoped for. It is only exceptions we can still experience under the best circumstances. From the *rule* that corruption is prevalent, that corruption is fatalistic, no God can save music.—

EPILOGUE

Let us finally, in order to take breath, withdraw for a moment from the narrow world to which all questions concerning the worth of *persons* condemn the mind. A philosopher requires to wash his hands after he has so long occupied himself with the "case of Wagner."—I give my conception of the *Modern.*—Every age has in its quantum of energy, a quantum determining what virtues are permitted to it, what virtues are proscribed. It has either the virtues of *ascending* life, and then it resists to the uttermost the virtues of descending life; or it is itself an epoch of descending life, and then it requires the virtues of decline, then it hates all that justifies itself solely by plenitude, by superabundance of strength. Æsthetics is indissolubly bound up with these biological presuppositions: there is *décadence* æsthetics, and there is *classical* æsthetics,—the "beautiful in itself" is a chimera, like all idealism.—In the narrower sphere of so-called moral values there is no greater contrast than that of *master morality* and morality according to *Christian* valuation: the latter grown up on a thoroughly morbid soil (the Gospels present to us precisely the same physiological types which the romances of Dostoyevsky depict); master morality ("Roman," "heathen," "classical," "Renaissance") reversely, as the symbolic language of well-constitutedness, of *ascending* life, of the will to power as the principle of life. Master morality *affirms,* just as instinctively as Christian morality *denies* ("God," "the other world," "self-renunciation"—nothing but negations). The former communicates to things out of its fullness—it glorifies, it embellishes, it *rationalises* the world, the latter impoverishes, blanches, and mars the value of things, it *denies* the world. "The world," a Christian term of insult. These antithetical forms in the optics of values are *both* indispensable: they are modes of seeing which one does not reach with reasons and refutations. One does not refute Christianity, one does not refute a disease of the eye. To have combated pessimism as one combats a philosophy was the acme of learned idiocy. The concepts "true" and "untrue" have not, as it seems to me, any meaning in optics.—That against which alone one has to defend one's self is the falsity, the instinctive duplicity, which *will* not be sensible of these antitheses as antitheses: as was the case with Wagner, for example, who possessed no little masterliness in such falsities. To look enviously towards master morality, *noble* morality (the Icelandic legend is almost its most important document), and at the same time to have in his mouth the contrary doctrine, the "Gospel of the Lowly," the *need* of salvation! . . . In passing, let me say that I admire the modesty of the Christians who go to Bayreuth. I myself should not endure certain words out of the mouth of Wagner. There are conceptions which do *not* belong to Bayreuth . . . What? A Christianity adjusted for Wagneriennes, perhaps *by* Wagneriennes (for Wagner in his old days was positively *feminini generis*)? Let me say once more that the Christians of to-day are too modest for me . . . If Wagner was a Christian, then Liszt was perhaps a Church-Father![8]—The need of *salvation,* the essence of all Christian needs, has nothing to do with such harlequins; it is the sincerest form of expression of *décadence,* the most convinced and most painful affirmation of it in sublime symbols and practices. The Christian wishes to get *loose* from himself. *Le moi est toujours haïssable.*—Noble morality, master morality, has, reversely, its roots in a triumphing *self* affirmation,—it is the self-affirming, the self-glorifying of life; it equally needs sublime symbols and practices, but only "because its heart is too full." All *beautiful* art, all *great* art belongs here: the essence of both is gratitude. On the other hand, one cannot discount from it an instinctive aversion from the *décadents,* a disdain, a horror even, before their symbolism: such is almost its demonstration. The noble Roman recognised Christianity as a *fœda superstitio;* I here remind you how Goethe, the last German of noble taste, felt with regard to the cross. One seeks in vain for more valuable, for more *indispensable* contrasts.[9]

But such a falsity as that of the Bayreuthians is now no exception. We all know the unæsthetic conception of the Christian "gentleman." Indeed that *innocence* in the midst of contradictions, that "good conscience" in lying, is *modern par excellence;* one almost defines modernism by it. Modern man represents biologically a *contradiction of moral values,* he sits between two chairs, he says in one breath, Yea and Nay. What wonder, then, that just in our time, falsity itself became flesh and even genius? what wonder that *Wagner* "dwelt among us?" It was not without reason that I named Wagner the Cagliostro of modernism . . . But we all, unconsciously and involuntarily, have in ourselves standards, phrases, formulae, and moralities of *contradictory* origin,—regarded physiologically, we are *spurious* . . . A *diagnostic of modern soul*—what would it commence with? With a resolute incision into this contradictoriness of instincts, with the disentangling of its antithetical moral values, with a vivisection performed on its *most instructive case.*—The case of Wagner is a *fortunate case* for the philosopher—this work, one hears, is inspired by gratitude . . .

---

[8] Liszt was Wagner's father-in-law.

[9] NOTE.—My "Genealogy of Morals" furnished the first information concerning the contrast between "*noble* morality" and "*Christian* morality; "there is perhaps no more decisive modification of thought in the history of religious and moral knowledge. That book, my touchstone for what belongs to me, has the good fortune to be accessible only to the most elevated and the most rigorous minds: *others* have not got ears for it. One has to have one's passion in things where nobody has it at present . . .

NIETZSCHE CONTRA WAGNER:

THE BRIEF OF A PSYCHOLOGIST

PREFACE

The following chapters are all rather carefully selected out of my older writings—some of them go back to 1877,—they are perhaps simplified here and there; above all, they are shortened. When read in succession, they will leave no doubt concerning either Richard Wagner or myself: we are antipodes Something further will also be understood: for example, that this is an essay for psychologists, but *not* for Germans . . . I have my readers everywhere, in Vienna, in St. Petersburg, in Copenhagen and Stockholm, in Paris, in New York—*I have not* them in Europe's Flatland, Germany . . . And I might perhaps also have a word to whisper in the ear of Messrs. the Italians, whom I love just as much as I . . . *Quousque tandem, Crispi* . . . *Triple alliance:* with the "Empire" an intelligent people will never make aught but a *mésalliance . . .*

Turin, Christmas-tide 1888.

Friedrich Nietzsche.

WHERE I ADMIRE

I believe artists often do not know what they can do best: they are too conceited for that. Their attention is directed to something prouder than those little plants give promise of, which know how to grow up in actual perfection, new, rare, and beautiful, on their soil. The final excellency of their own garden and vineyard is superficially estimated by them, and their love and their insight are not of equal quality. There is a musician, who, more than any other, has the genius for finding the tones peculiar to suffering, oppressed, tortured souls, and even for giving speech to dumb misery. No one equals him in the colours of the late autumn, the indescribably pathetic happiness of a last, alder-last, alder-shortest enjoyment; he knows a sound for those (secretly haunted midnights of the soul when cause and effect seem to have gone out of joint and every instant something can originate out of nothing. He draws his resources best of all out of the lowest depth of human happiness, and as it were out of its drained goblet, where the bitterest and most nauseous drops have at the end—the good or the bad end—met with the sweetest. He knows that weary self-impelling of the soul which can no longer leap or fly, yea, not even walk; he has the shy glance of pain that is concealed, of understanding without comfort, of leave-taking without confession; yea, as the Orpheus of all secret misery, he is greater than anyone, and much has been added to art through him only, much which was hitherto inexpressible and even seemingly unworthy of art—the cynical revolts, for example, of which only the greatest sufferers are capable, and likewise many quite small and microscopic matters belonging to the soul, as it were the scales of its amphibious nature,—yes, he is the *master* of minutiæ. But he does not *wish* to be so! His character loves rather the large walls and the audacious wall-painting . . . He fails to observe that his spirit has a different taste and inclination—antithetical *optics,*—and likes best of all to sit quietly in the corners of broken-down houses: concealed there, concealed from himself, he paints his proper masterpieces, which are all very short, often only one measure in length,—it is not till there that he becomes quite good, great, and perfect, perhaps there only.—Wagner is one who has suffered sorely—that is his *pre-eminence* over the other musicians. I admire Wagner in everything in which he sets *himself* to music.—

WHERE I MAKE OBJECTIONS

That is not to say that I regard this music as healthy, and there least of all where it speaks of Wagner. My objections to Wagner's music are physiological objections: for what purpose is to be served by disguising the same under aesthetic formulae? Æsthetics is certainly nothing but applied Physiology.—My "matter of fact" my "*petit fait vrai,*" is that I no longer breathe easily when once this music operates on me, that my *foot* immediately becomes angry at it and revolts: my foot has need of measure, dance, march—even the young German Kaiser cannot march according to Wagner's Kaiser-march,—my foot desires first of all from music the raptures which lie in *good* walking, stepping, and dancing. But does not my stomach also protest? my heart? my circulation? do not my bowels fret? Do I not unawares become hoarse thereby . . . In order to listen to Wagner I need *pastilles Géraudel* . . . And so I ask myself, what is it at all that my whole body specially *wants* from music? *For* there is no soul . . . I believe it wants *alleviation:* as if all the animal functions were to be accelerated by light, bold, wanton, self-assured rhythms; as if iron, leaden life were to lose its heaviness by golden, tender, unctuous melodies. My melancholy wants to take its repose in the hiding-places and abysses of *perfection:* for that purpose I need music. But Wagner makes people morbid.—Of what account is the theatre to *me?* The convulsions of its "moral" ecstasies in which the mob—and who is not "mob!"—has its satisfaction? The whole pantomime hocus-pocus of the stage-player?—It is obvious that I am essentially antitheatrically constituted: I have, from the bottom of my soul, for the theatre—this *art of the masses par excellence*—that profound scorn which at present every artist has. *Success* in the theatre—a person thereby sinks in my estimation, till he is never again seen; *non-success*—then I prick up my ears and begin to esteem . . . But Wagner was the reverse (*besides* the Wagner who had made the lonesomest of all music), essentially a theatre man and stage-player, perhaps the most enthusiastic mimo-maniac that has existed, *even as a musician* . . . And in passing, we would say that if it has been Wagner's theory, "the drama is the end, music is always but the means,"—his *praxis,* on the contrary, from the beginning to the close, has been, "the attitude is the end, the drama, as well as music, is always only the means." Music as a means for elucidating, strengthening, and internalising the dramatic pantomime and stage-player concreteness; and the Wagnerian drama only an occasion for many interesting attitudes!—He possessed, along with all the other instincts, the *commanding* instincts of a great stage-player in all and everything: and, as we have said, also as a musician.—I once made this clear, not without *trouble,* to a Wagnerian *pur sang,*—clearness and Wagnerians! I do not say a word more. There was reason for adding further—"Be but a little more honest with yourself! for we are not in Bayreuth. In Bayreuth people are only honest in the mass, as individuals they lie, they deceive themselves. They leave themselves at home when they go to Bayreuth, they renounce the right to their own tongue and choice, to their taste, even to their courage, as they have it and use it within their own four walls with respect to God and the world. Nobody takes the most refined sentiments of his art into the theatre with him, least of all the artist who works for the theatre,—solitude is wanting, the perfect does not tolerate witnesses. In the theatre one becomes mob, herd, woman, Pharisee, voting animal, patron, idiot—

Wagnerian: there even the most personal conscience succumbs to the levelling charm of the great multitude, there the neighbour rules, there one *becomes* neighbour . . ."

WAGNER AS A DANGER

1

The object which recent music pursues in what is at present called—by a strong though obscure name—"infinite melody" one can explain to one's self by going into the sea, gradually losing secure footing on the bottom, and finally submitting one's self to the element at discretion: one has to *swim.* In older music, in an elegant, or solemn, or passionate to-and-fro, faster and slower, one had to do something quite different, namely, to *dance.* The proportion necessary thereto, the observance of definite balance in measures of time and intensity, extorted from the soul of the hearer a continuous *consideration,*—on the contrast between this cooler breeze, which originated from consideration, and the breath of enthusiasm warmed through, the charm of all *good* music rested.—Richard Wagner wanted another kind of movement—he overthrew the physiological pre-requisite of previous music. Swimming, hovering—no longer walking, dancing . . . Perhaps the decisive word is thereby said. "Infinite melody" just *seeks* to break up all symmetry of measure and intensity, at times it derides it even—it has its wealth of invention precisely in what sounded to the ears of former times as rhythmical paradox and abuse. Out of an imitation, out of a predominance of such a taste, there might arise such a danger to music that a greater could not even be imagined—the complete degeneration of "rhythmical feeling, *chaos* in place of rhythm . . . The danger reaches its climax when such a music rests always more and more upon entirely naturalistic stage-playing and pantomime, which, subject to no law of plastic art, desire *effect* and nothing more . . . The *espressivo* at any price, and music in the service, in the slavery of attitude—*that is the end . . .*

2

What? would it really be the first virtue of a performance (as the performing musical artists at present seem to believe), to attain under all circumstances a *haut-relief* which cannot be surpassed? Is not this, when applied, for example, to Mozart, the special sin against the spirit of Mozart, the gay, enthusiastic, tender, amorous spirit of Mozart, who, fortunately, was not German, and whose seriousness is a gracious, golden seriousness, and *not* that of a German Philistine . . . Not to mention the seriousness of the "marble statue" . . . But you think that *all* music is music of the "marble statue,"—that *all* music must spring forth out of the wall and agitate the hearer to his very bowels . . . It is only thus that music is said to operate!—*Who* is there operated upon? Something on which a *noble* artist must never operate,—the masses! the immature! the used up! the morbid! the idiots! the *Wagnerians! . . .*

A MUSIC WITHOUT A FUTURE

Music, of all the arts that know how to grow up on the soil of a certain civilisation, makes its appearance last of the plants, perhaps because it is the most intrinsic, and consequently arrives latest—in the autumn and withering of each civilisation. It was only in the art of the Dutch masters that the soul of the Christian Middle Ages found its dying echo,—their tone-architecture is the posthumous, though genuine and equally legitimate sister of Gothic. It was only in Handel's music that the best re-echoed out of the soul of Luther and his kin: the heroic Jewish trait, which gave the Reformation a touch of greatness,—the Old Testament become music, *not* the New Testament. It was reserved for Mozart to pay in clinking gold pieces the balance due to the age of Louis XIV and the art of Racine and Claude Lorrain; it was only in Beethoven's and Rossini's music that the eighteenth century sang itself out, the century of enthusiasm, of broken ideals, and of *fugitive* happiness. All true, all original music is a swan's song.—Perhaps even our latest" music, notwithstanding its predominance and ambition, has but a brief space of time before it; for it originated out of a civilisation whose basis is rapidly sinking,—a forthwith *sunken* civilisation. A certain Catholicism of sentiment, and a delight in some ancient indigenous (so-called "national") existence, or nuisance, are its pre-requisites. Wagner's appropriation of old legends and songs in which learned prejudice had taught us to see something Germanic *par excellence*—we laugh at that now,—and the new inspiration of these Scandinavian monsters with a thirst for ecstatic sensuality and super-sensuality: all this taking and giving of Wagner in respect to materials, characters, passions, and nerves, would also express plainly the *spirit of Wagner's music,* provided that this itself, like all music, should not know how to speak unambiguously of itself: fox music is a *woman* . . . We must not allow ourselves to be misled with regard to this state of affairs by the fact that for the moment we are living precisely in the reaction *within* the reaction. The age of national wars, of ultramontane martyrdom, this whole *interlude*-character which the circumstances of Europe at present are possessed of, may, in fact, assist such art as that of Wagner in obtaining a sudden glory, without thereby guaranteeing to it a future. The Germans themselves have no future . . .

WE ANTIPODES

It will be remembered perhaps, at least among my friends, that at the commencement I rushed upon this modern world with some errors and overestimates, and in any case as a *hopeful person.* I understood—who knows from what personal experiences?—the philosophical pessimism of the nineteenth century as the symptom of a higher thinking power, of a more triumphal fullness of life than had found expression in the philosophy of Hume, Kant, and Hegel,—I took *tragical* perception for the choicest luxury of our civilisation, as its most precious, most noble, most dangerous mode of squandering, but always, on the ground of its superabundance, as its *permitted* luxury.

I similarly interpreted Wagner's music in my own way, as the expression of a Dionysian powerfulness of soul, I believed that I heard in it the earthquake with which a primitive force of life, suppressed for ages, finally relieves itself, indifferent as to whether all that at present calls itself civilisation is shaken thereby. It is obvious what I misunderstood, it is obvious in like manner what I *bestowed upon* Wagner and Schopenhauer—myself . . . Every art, every philosophy may be regarded as a medicine and helping expedient of advancing or decaying life: they always presuppose suffering and sufferers. But there are two kinds of sufferers: on the one hand those suffering from the *superabundance* of life, who want a Dionysian art and similarly a tragic insight and prospect with regard to life,—and on the other hand those suffering from the *impoverishment* of life, who desire repose, stillness, smooth sea, *or else* ecstasy, convulsion, intoxication furnished by art and philosophy. The revenge on life itself—the most voluptuous kind of ecstasy for such impoverished ones! . . . To the double requirement of the latter Wagner, just like Schopenhauer, corresponds—they both deny life, they calumniate it; they are thereby my antipodes.—The richest in fullness of life, the Dionysian God and man, may not only allow himself the spectacle of the frightful and the questionable, but even the frightful deed, and every luxury of destruction, decomposition and denial,—with him the evil, the senseless, and the loathsome appear as it were permitted, as they appear to be permitted in nature—as a consequence of the superabundance of the procreative, restorative powers—which out of every desert is still able to create a luxuriant orchard. On the other hand those suffering most, the poorest in life, would have most need of gentleness, peaceableness, and benevolence—that which at present is called humanity—in thinking as well as in practice: if possible, a God who is quite specially a God for the sick, a *"Heiland;"* similarly also logic, the understandableness of existence as a conception, even for idiots—the typical "freethinkers," like the "idealists," and "beautiful souls," are all *décadents;* in short, a certain warm, fear-excluding narrowness and inclusion in optimistic horizons which permit *stupefaction* . . . In this manner, I gradually learned to understand Epicurus, the antithesis of a Dionysian Greek; in like manner the Christian, who, in fact, is only a species of Epicurean who, with the doctrine, "belief makes *blessed*," carries out the principle of Hedonism *as far as possible*—till he is beyond all intellectual righteousness . . . If I have something in advance of all psychologists, it is that my insight is sharper for that nicest and most insidious species of *inference a posteriori* in which most errors are made: the inference from the work to its originator, from the deed to the doer, from the ideal to him who *needs* it, from every mode of thinking and valuing to the ruling *requirement* behind it.—In respect to artists of every kind, I now make use of this main distinction: has the *hatred* of life, or the *superabundance* of life, become creative here? In Goethe, for example, the superabundance became creative, in Flaubert the hatred: Flaubert, a new edition of Pascal, but as an artist with instinctive judgment at bottom: *"Flaubert est toujours haïssable, l'homme n'est rien, l'œuvre est tout"* . . . He tortured himself when he composed, quite as Pascal tortured himself when he thought—they both felt "unegotistic." "Unselfishness"—the *décadence*-principle, the will to the end in art as well as in morals.

WHERE WAGNER BELONGS TO

Even at the present time France is still the seat of the most intellectual and refined civilisation of Europe, and the *high* school of taste: but one must know how to find this "France of taste." The *Norddeutsche Zeitung,* for example, or he who has it for his mouthpiece, sees in the French, "barbarians,"—as for me, I seek for the *black* part of earth, where "the slaves" ought to be freed, in the neighbourhood of the *Norddeutsche* . . . He who belongs to *that* France keeps himself well concealed: there may be a small number in whom it is embodied and lives, besides perhaps men who do not stand upon the strongest legs, in part fatalistic, melancholy, sick, in part over-pampered, over-refined, such as have the *ambition* to be artificial—but they have in their possession all the elevation and delicacy that is still left in the world. In this France of intellect, which is also the France of pessimism, Schopenhauer is at present more at home than he ever has been in Germany; his principal work twice translated already, the second time admirably, so that I now prefer to read Schopenhauer in French (he was an *accident* among Germans, as I am an accident—the Germans have no fingers for us, they have no fingers at all, they have only claws). Not to speak of Heinrich Heine—*l'adorable Heine* they say in Paris—who has long ago passed over into the flesh and blood of the profounder and more soul-breathing lyric poets of France. What would German horned cattle know of how to deal with the *délicatesses* of such a nature!—Finally, as regards Richard Wagner: one would seize it with hands, not perhaps with fists, that Paris is the proper *soil* for Wagner: the more French music shapes itself according to the needs of the "*âme moderne,*" the more it becomes Wagnerian,—it already does so sufficiently.—One must not allow one's self to be misled here by Wagner himself—it was sheer wickedness of Wagner to mock at Paris in its agony in 1871 . . . In Germany Wagner is nevertheless a mere misunderstanding: who would be more incapable of understanding anything of Wagner than the young Kaiser, for example?—The fact remains certain, nevertheless, for everyone who is acquainted with the movement of European civilisation, that French Romanticism and Richard Wagner are very closely connected. Altogether dominated by literature, up to their eyes and ears—the first artists of Europe possessing a *universal literary* culture,—mostly even themselves writers, poets, intermediaries and blenders of the senses and arts, altogether fanatics of *expression,* great discoverers in the domain of the sublime, also of the loathsome and the shocking, still greater discoverers in effect, in display, in the art of the shop window, altogether talented far beyond their geniuses,— *virtuosi* through and through with dismal accesses to everything which seduces, allures, forces, or upsets, born enemies of logic and the straight line, covetous of the foreign, the exotic, the monstrous, and all opiates of the senses and understanding. On the whole, a rashly-venturing, magnificently-violent, high-flying, and high up-pulling kind of artists, who had first to teach to *their* century—it is the century of the *mass*—the conception of "artist." But *sick* . . .

WAGNER AS THE APOSTLE OF CHASTITY

1

    —Is this our mode?
From German heart came this vexed ululating?
From German body this self-lacerating?
Is ours this priestly hand-dilation,
 This incense-fuming excitation?
Is ours this plunging, faltering, brangling,
This, sweet as sugar, ding-dong-dangling?
This sly nun ogling, Ave-hour-bell tinkled,
This whole false rapturous flight beyond the heavens star-sprinkled? . . .

    —Is this our mode?
Think well! Ye still stay for ingression . . .
For what ye hear is *Rome,—Rome's faith without expression.*

2

Chastity and sensuality are not necessarily antithetical; every true marriage, every genuine love-affair is beyond any such antithesis. But in those cases in which this antithesis really exists, it fortunately needs not at all to be a tragical antithesis. This might at least be the case with all better constituted, more cheerful mortals, who are not at all disposed, without further ado, to reckon their fluctuating state of equilibrium betwixt angel and *petite bête* among the arguments against existence,—the finest, the brightest, such as Hafiz and Goethe, have even discerned an additional charm therein. It is just such contradictions that allure to life . . . But if, on the other hand, the ill-constituted beasts of Circe can be induced to worship chastity, they will, as is but too plain, see and *worship* in it only their own antithesis—and oh, one can imagine with how much tragic grunting and eagerness!—that same painful and absolutely superfluous antithesis which Richard Wagner at the end of his days undoubtedly intended to set to music and produce on the stage. *For what purpose really?* we may reasonably ask.

3

Here, to be sure, that other question cannot be avoided: what had Wagner really to do with that manly (alas, so very unmanly) "rustic simplicity," the poor devil and country lad, Parsifal, whom, by such insidious means, he finally succeeded in making a Roman Catholic—what? was this Parsifal really meant *seriously?* For that people have *laughed* over him I would least of all dispute, nor would Gottfried Keller do so . . . One might wish that the Wagnerian *Parsifal* had been meant to be gay, like a finale or satiric drama, with which, precisely in a due and worthy manner, the tragedian Wagner had intended to take his farewell of us, also of himself, and above all *of tragedy,* namely, with an excess of the greatest and most wanton parody on the tragical itself, on all the awful earth-earnestness and earth-sorrowfulness of the past, on the *stupidest* form of the antinaturalness of the ascetic ideal finally surmounted. For *Parsifal* is an operetta theme *par excellence* . . . Are we to understand Wagner's *Parsifal* as his secret laugh of superiority at himself, as the triumph of his greatest, finally attained artistic freedom and artistic other-worldness—Wagner, who knows how to *laugh* at himself? . . . As has been said, one might wish that it were so: for what sense could we attach to a *Parsifal seriously meant?* Is it really necessary to suppose (as I have been told) that Wagner's *Parsifal* is "the product of a maddened hatred of perception, intellect, and sensuality?" an anathema on sense and intellect in one breath, in a fit of hatred? an apostasy and return to sickly, Christian, and obscurantist ideals? And finally, worst of all, the self-negation and self-annulment of an artist who had striven so far, with all his will-power, for the opposite, namely, for the highest spiritualising and sensualising of his art? And not only of his art, but of his life as well. Let us recollect how enthusiastically Wagner once walked in the footsteps of Feuerbach the philosopher. Feuerbach's phrase of "a healthy sensuality," echoed in the third and fourth decades of this century to Wagner as to many other Germans—they called themselves the *young* Germans—like the word of salvation. Did the older Wagner *unlearn* his former creed? Very likely he did! judging from the disposition he evinced toward the end of his life to *unteach* his first belief . . . Has the *hatred of life* got the upper hand in him, as in Flaubert? . . . For *Parsifal* is a work of cunning, of revengefulness, of secret poison-brewing, hostile to the pre-requisites of life;

a *bad* work.—The preaching of chastity is an incitement to antinaturalness: I despise everyone who does not regard *Parsifal* as an outrage on morals.—

HOW I GOT FREE FROM WAGNER

1

As far back as the summer of 1876, in the middle of the period of the first festival plays, my heart had taken farewell of Wagner. I cannot stand anything ambiguous; and since Wagner's return to Germany, he had condescended step by step to everything that I despise—even to Anti-Semitism . . . It was, in fact, high time to take farewell then: soon enough I got proof of that. Richard Wagner, apparently the most triumphal, while in truth become a decayed, despairing *décadent,* sank down suddenly, helpless and disjointed, before the Christian cross . . . Was there no German then with eyes in his head, or sympathy in his conscience, for this awe-inspiring spectacle? Was I the only one who— *suffered* from it?—Enough; to myself the unexpected event, like a flash of lightning, illuminated the position I had left,—and also that subsequent horror which everyone feels who has passed unconsciously through a fearful danger. When I went further on alone, I shivered; not long thereafter I was sick, more than sick, namely, *fatigued:*—fatigued by the incessant undeceiving concerning all that yet remained for the inspiration of us modern men, concerning the strength, labour, hope, youth, and love *squandered* on all sides; fatigued out of disgust for the whole idealistic falsity and softening of conscience, which here once more had scored a victory over one of the bravest; fatigued, finally, and not least, by the grief of an unrelenting suspicion—that I was henceforth condemned to mistrust more profoundly, to depise more profoundly, to be more profoundly *alone,* than ever before. For I had had no one but Richard Wagner . . . I was *condemned* perpetually to the Germans . . .

2

Lonely, henceforth, and sadly mistrustful of myself, I then, not without indignation, took sides *against* myself, and *for* everything which gave pain to, and was hard upon me; I thus found the way again to that brave pessimism which is the antithesis of all idealistic falsity, and also, as it would appear to me, the way to *myself*—to *my* task . . . That concealed and imperious something for which for a long time we have had no name, until it finally proves itself to be our task,—this tyrant in us retaliates frightfully for every attempt which we make to shirk it or escape from it, for every premature decision, for every thinking ourselves equal to those of whose number we are not, for every activity, however honourable it may be, if it happen to distract us from our main business—nay, even for every virtue which might shield us from the sternness of our special responsibility. Sickness is always the answer, when we are inclined to doubt concerning our right to *our* task, when we begin to make it easier for ourselves in any respect. Strange and frightful at the same time! It is our *alleviations* for which we must do the severest penance! And if we want afterwards to return to health, there is no choice for us: we must burden ourselves *heavier* than we were ever burdened before . . .

THE PSYCHOLOGIST SPEAKS

1

The more a psychologist, a born, an unavoidable psychologist and soul-diviner, turns his attention to the more select cases and individuals, the greater becomes his danger of suffocation by sympathy. He *needs* sternness and gaiety more than another man. For corruption, the ruin of higher men, is the rule: it is dreadful to have such a rule always before one's eyes. The manifold tortures of the psychologist who has once discovered this ruin, and has then in *almost* every case throughout all history discovered this entire internal "unblessedness" of higher man, this eternal "too late!" in every sense—may perhaps one day become the cause of his own *ruin* . . . One perceives, in almost every psychologist, a tell-tale preference for intercourse with common and well-ordered men, such as betrays that he always requires curing, that he needs a sort of flight and forgetfulness away from what his insight, his incisions, his *business* have laid upon his conscience. He is possessed by a fear of his memory. He is easily silenced before the judgment of others, he hears with unmoved countenance how others reverence, admire, love, and glorify where he has *perceived,*—or he even conceals his silence by expressing his agreement with some superficial opinion. Perhaps the paradox of his situation gets to be so horrible that the "educated classes," on their part, learn great reverence precisely where he has learned *great sympathy* and *great contempt* . . . And who knows if in all great cases nothing more than this took place,—that a God was worshipped, and the God was only a poor sacrificial animal . . . *Success* has always been the greatest liar—and the *work,* the *deed* is a success as well . . . The great statesman, the conqueror, the discoverer, are disguised in their creations, hidden away until they are unrecognisable; the work of the artist, of the philosopher, only invents him who has created it, *is said* to have created it . . . The "great men," as they are reverenced, are poor little fictions composed afterwards,—in the world of historical values spurious coinage is *current* . . .

2

Those great poets, for example, such as Byron, Musset, Poe, Leopardi, Kleist, Gogol—I do not venture to name much greater names, but I think them—as they avowedly are and must be, men of the moment, sensuous, absurd, five-fold, light-minded, and hasty in mistrust and in trust; with souls in which usually some flaw has to be concealed; often taking revenge by their works for an inner contamination, often seeking forgetfulness with their upward flights from a too-true memory, idealists out of the neighbourhood of the *swamp*—what torments these great artists are, and the so-called higher men generally, for him who has once found them out . . . We are all advocates of the mediocre . . . It is conceivable that it is just from woman (who is clairvoyant in the world of suffering, and alas, also, ready to help and save to an extent far beyond her powers) that *they* experience so easily those outbreaks of unlimited sympathy, which the multitude, above all the *reverent* multitude, overloads with inquisitive and self-satisfying interpretations. This sympathising deceives itself constantly as to its power: woman would like to believe that love can do *all,*—it is a *superstition* peculiar to herself. Alas, he who knows the heart finds out how poor, helpless, pretentious, and liable to error even the best, the deepest love is—how it rather *destroys* than saves . . .

3

The intellectual loathing and haughtiness of any man who has suffered profoundly—it almost determines rank, *how* profoundly a person can suffer,—the chilling certainty, with which he is entirely imbued and coloured, that in virtue of his suffering he *knows more* than the shrewdest and wisest could know, that he has been familiar with, and at home in many distant, frightful worlds, of which "*you* know nothing" . . . this tacit intellectual haughtiness, this pride of the elect of perception, of the "initiated," of the almost sacrificed, deems all kinds of disguises necessary to protect itself from contact with over-officious and sympathising hands, and, in general, from all that is not its equal in suffering. Profound suffering makes noble; it separates.—One of the most refined forms of disguise is Epicurism, and a certain ostentatious boldness of taste, which takes the suffering lightly, and puts itself in defence against all that is sorrowful and profound. There are "gay men" who make use of gaiety, because, on account of it, they are misunderstood,—they *wish* to be misunderstood. There are "scientific minds," which make use of science, because it gives a gay appearance and because the scientific spirit suggests that a person is superficial—they wish to mislead to a false conclusion . . . There are free, insolent minds which would fain conceal and deny that at the bottom they are disjointed, incurable souls—it is the case of Hamlet: and then folly itself may be the mask for an unhappy *over-assured* knowledge.—

EPILOGUE

1

I have often asked myself if I am not under deeper obligation to the hardest years of my life than to any other. As my innermost nature teaches me, all that is necessary, when viewed from an elevation and in the sense of a *great* economy, is also the useful in itself,—one should not only bear it, one should *love* it . . . *Amor fati:* that is my innermost nature.—And as regards my long sickness, do I not owe to it unutterably more than to my health? I owe to it a *higher* health, such a health as becomes stronger by everything that does not kill it! *I owe to it also my philosophy* . . . It is great affliction only that is the ultimate emancipator of the mind, as the instructor of *strong suspicion* which makes an X out of every U, a true, correct X, that is, the penultimate letter of the alphabet, before the last . . . It is great affliction only—that long, slow affliction in which we are burned as it were with green wood, which takes time,—that compels us philosophers to descend into our ultimate depth and divest ourselves of all trust, all good-nature, glossing, gentleness, and averageness, where we have perhaps formerly installed our humanity. I doubt whether such affliction "improves" us: but I know that it *deepens* us . . . Be it that we learn to confront it with our pride, our scorn, our strength of will, doing like the Indian who, however sorely he may be tortured, takes revenge on his tormentor by his bad tongue; be it that We withdraw from affliction into nothingness, into dumb, benumbed, deaf self-surrender, self-forgetfulness, and self-extinction;—from such long, dangerous exercises of self-mastery one emerges as another man, with several *additional* interrogation marks,—above all, with the will to question henceforward more, more profoundly, more strictly, more sternly, more wickedly, more quietly than has ever been questioned on earth before . . . Confidence in life is gone; life itself has become a *problem.*—May it never be believed that one has thereby necessarily become a gloomy person, a moping owl! Even love to life is still possible,—only one loves *differently* . . . It is the love to a woman that causes us doubts . . .

2

The strangest thing is this: one has afterwards another taste,—a *second* taste. Out of such abysses, including the abyss of *strong suspicion,* one comes back born again, with the skin cast, more ticklish, more wicked, with a finer taste for pleasure, with a more delicate tongue for all good things, with a merrier disposition, with a second and more dangerous innocence in pleasure, more childish and also a hundred times more refined than one had ever been before.

Oh, how repugnant to one henceforth is gratification, coarse, dull, drab-coloured gratification, as usually understood by those who enjoy life, our "educated" class, our rich and ruling class! How malignantly we now listen to the great bum-bum of the fair with which (by means of art, book, and music and with the assistance of spirituous liquors) "educated" people and city men at present allow themselves to be outraged for the sake of "intellectual gratification!" How the theatre-cry of passion now pains our ear, how the whole romantic tumult and sensuous hubbub which the educated mob love (together with its aspirations after the sublime, the elevated, the preposterous), has become strange to our. taste! No, if we convalescents still need an art, it is *another* art—an ironical, easy, fugitive, divinely untrammelled, divinely artificial art, which, like a pure flame, blazes forth in an unclouded heaven! Above all, an art for artists, *only for artists!* We afterwards understand better about what is first of all necessary thereto: gaiety, *all* gaiety, my friends! . . . We know some things too well now, we knowing ones: oh, how we henceforth learn to forget well, things well *not* to know, as artists! . . . And as regards our future: we will scarcely be found again on the paths of those Egyptian youths who at night make the temples unsafe, embrace statues, and absolutely want to unveil, uncover, and put into clear light everything which for good reasons is kept concealed. No, this bad taste, this will to truth, to "truth at any price," this madness of youths in the love of truth—has become disagreeable to us: for it we are too experienced, too serious, too jovial, too shrewd, too *profound* . . . We no longer believe that truth remains truth when the veil is pulled off it,—we have lived long enough to believe this . . . At present it is regarded as a matter of propriety not to be anxious to see everything naked, to be present at everything, to understand and "know" everything. *Tout comprendre—c'est tout mépriser* . . . "Is it true that God is everywhere present?" asked a little girl of her mother; "that is indecent, I think"—a hint to philosophers! . . . One ought to have more reverence for the *bashfulness* with which nature has concealed herself behind enigmas and variegated uncertainties. Is truth perhaps a woman who has reasons *for not showing her reasons?* . . . Is her name perhaps, to speak in Greek, *Baubo?* . . . Oh these Greeks! they knew how to *live!* For that end it is necessary, to remain bravely at the surface, the fold, the skin, to worship appearance, to believe in forms, in tones, in words, in the whole *Olympus of appearance!* These Greeks were superficial—*out of profundity* . . . And do we not just come back thereto, we adventurers of intellect, we who have climbed up the highest and most dangerous peak of present thought and have looked around us therefrom, we who have *looked down* therefrom? Are we not just therein—Greeks? Worshippers of forms, of tones, and of words? and just by virtue of that—*artists?* . . .

www.ingramcontent.com/pod-product-compliance
Lightning Source LLC
Chambersburg PA
CBHW030314030426
42337CB00012B/699